*◆ FIRST ◆ ACTION ◆ SKILLS ◆*

# Soccer

## Bridget Gibbs

Soccer consultant:  Barney Jones, Football Development
Officer, Newcastle-upon-Tyne

## Contents

Action photography by Chris Gilbert
Soccer advice also given by Michael Gibson of Gosforth Park
First School
Illustrated by Guy Smith

The publishers would like to thank all those who gave their assistance in making this book, and especially David Cooper, Peter Stewart, Nathan Barnes, Lee Charlton, Sarah  Leavey, Amanda Logan, Robin Grey and Hannah Gittos for acting as models.

# INTRODUCING SOCCER

Soccer is the most popular team game in the world. In the biggest of the international competitions, the World Cup, more than 160 nations take part (see page 5). The final match of this knock-out competition is watched by millions of people.

The great advantage of soccer is that you do not need any special equipment to start playing – just an open space, a ball, something to mark goal posts and a group of friends. You can even practise by yourself.

Diego Maradona of Argentina parades Soccer's most prized trophy, the World Cup. ▼

## ABOUT THIS BOOK

This book explains all about soccer and how it is played. It contains lots of practice ideas to help you develop basic playing skills, and you can also find out about the rules of the game and what it's like to be a professional player.

**Soccer is played by both girls and boys.**

## How soccer started

A form of soccer was played by the Chinese more than 2,000 years ago, and the Romans are known to have played a version, too. They introduced it to England, where it became a popular and rowdy sport, often played by crowds of people in village streets.

In the 19th century, The Football Association was formed in England and a set of rules was established. Soccer soon spread throughout the world.

# PLAYING SOCCER

In a soccer game two teams of eleven players play against each other for 90 minutes. A referee controls the match, which is divided into two halves of 45 minutes with a break of 10 minutes in the middle.

The team captains toss a coin and the winner can decide whether his team will take the kick-off from the centre spot to start the match or choose which goal to attack first.

The aim of the game is to score as many goals as possible. The team with the ball tries to take it up the pitch to make an attempt at goal. The other team tries to get the ball by cutting off passes or tackling. Once they win the ball, they try to move up the pitch to take a shot at their opponent's goal.

When a team scores, play starts again with the other team kicking off from the centre spot. At half-time the teams change ends.

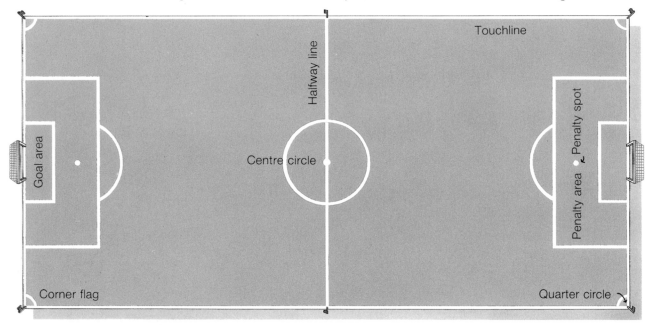

Touchline

Halfway line

Goal area

Centre circle

Penalty spot

Penalty area

Corner flag

Quarter circle

Pitch sizes vary, but they are all marked out as shown above. They should be no less than 90m (100yds) long and 45m (50yds) wide.

The goal and penalty areas are a standard size on all pitches. The width of the lines and the goal posts must not exceed 127mm (5″).

Each team is split into two elements: attack and defence. They can play in various different positions chosen by the manager.

## Starting to play

Young soccer players usually start off by playing matches of 20, 30 or 35 minutes in each half. When you first start, a small pitch with 5-, 6- or 7-a-side teams is best. You will get more chances to play the ball and so gain more experience.

**A 6-a-side game.**

## Clubs and competitions

In most countries professional soccer clubs are organized in a league in which teams of similar standards are grouped in divisions.

There are three other types of professional competition: national knock-out cups, European competitions for club teams and international competitions for competing countries.

### Club competitions

**Cup knock-outs:** Clubs from one country play each other in knock-out rounds.

**European Cup:** A knock-out competition between national league champions.

**European Cup-winner's Cup:** A knock-out competition between national cup-winners .

**UEFA Cup:** A knock-out tournament between leading clubs who have not qualified for the other competitions.

### International competitions

**European Championship:** A four-yearly competition between international teams.

**World Cup:** A four-yearly competition open to any country belonging to FIFA, the Federation of International Football Associations.

**Olympic Games:** Soccer has been played in the Olympic Games since 1900, between teams from different nations.

# SOCCER KIT

The most important part of your kit is your footwear. When you play on concrete, tarmac or synthetic (plastic) pitches, trainers are best.

However, when you start to play matches on grass pitches, you will need proper soccer boots with studs on the soles, to give a good grip on the pitch surface.

## Boots

Soccer boots are made of leather or synthetic material on man-made soles, with studs on the heel and sole areas. They also have long tongues to help protect the front of your ankle.

There are two types of boots: some have moulded studs that are part of the sole; others have separate screw-in studs.

**Tie laces firmly round the boot, making a bow and tucking loops in.**

## Boot studs

Moulded boot studs are best on hard pitches, whereas screw-in studs can be varied to suit any conditions. On a muddy pitch, slightly longer studs are best.

You can use a boot stud spanner to tighten or replace screw-in studs.

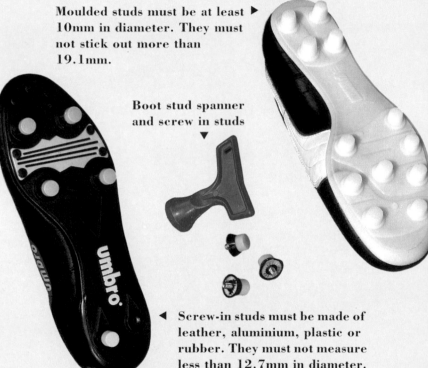

**Moulded studs must be at least ▶ 10mm in diameter. They must not stick out more than 19.1mm.**

**Boot stud spanner and screw in studs ▼**

**◀ Screw-in studs must be made of leather, aluminium, plastic or rubber. They must not measure less than 12.7mm in diameter.**

## Boot care

Always clean your boots after use. Scrape the mud off with a blunt knife, then wipe them over with a damp cloth before polishing.

## Team strip

When you play for a school or club team, you are likely to wear shorts, shirt and socks in the colours of your team. This is called the team strip.

**Shirts can have long or short sleeves. They sometimes have numbers on the back to identify the players' positions.**

**Shorts need to be fairly loose to allow easy movement.**

**Shin pads prevent cuts and bruises.**

**Goalkeepers wear a different colour from the rest of their team.**

**Gloves help protect goalkeepers' fingers when saving powerful shots, and give them a better grip when the ball is slippery.**

## Footballs

Footballs are made of leather or a waterproof man-made material. There are three sizes: 3,4 and 5.

Size 5 is used by players from the age of about 15 upwards. Size 4 is used by junior players, and size 3 is used by small children just learning about the game.

**The ball needs to be pumped up hard, using a football pump or a bicycle pump with a special adaptor.**

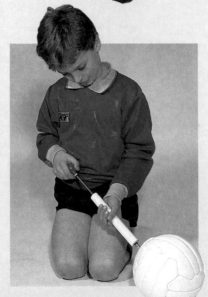

# PLAYERS AND POSITIONS

In a full-size soccer game each team has eleven players, wearing the numbers 1 to 11 on the backs of their shirts. There are four main types of players, explained on this page.

The number of defenders and attackers varies. It depends on the particular strengths of the team members and the decision of the team manager. The arrangement of players on the pitch is called the formation.

**An attacking 4-2-4 team formation**

## Defenders

The job of defenders, or backs, is to win the ball. They must be good at tackling, intercepting passes and heading. In some teams an extra defender, called a sweeper, plays behind the normal defenders.

## Strikers

Strikers need good shooting and heading skills to score goals. They must be able to kick with either foot and dribble well.

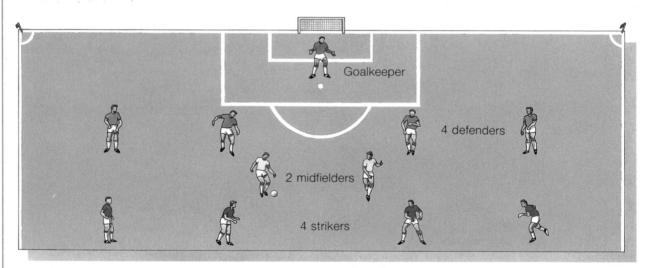

Goalkeeper

4 defenders

2 midfielders

4 strikers

## Midfield

These players defend and attack, depending on the situation. They play in midfield and have a lot of ground to cover, so they must be very fit. They need good passing skills, ball control and dribbling ability.

## Goalkeeper

Only one goalkeeper plays in a team. He is there to keep the ball out of the goal, so he must be alert and quick. He also organizes his team's defence  as he faces down the pitch and gets the best view of play.

## Other formations

Formations are listed from the back. They do not include the goalkeeper.

The 4-2-4 formation, shown on page 8 is the most attacking arrangement. The other three main formations are shown below.

**4-3-3.** An attacking line-up with 3 strikers, 3 midfielders and 4 defenders

**4-4-2.** A defensive line-up, with 4 defenders, 4 midfielders and 2 strikers.

**Sweeper system: The most defensive line-up. An extra player plays behind the defenders.**

## Team back-up

The *manager* chooses the team members for each match. He decides which tactics to use, and whether to substitute players during a game. He will watch the game from either the stand or the dug-out.

The *coach* organizes training sessions and helps the manager to decide on team tactics.

The *physiotherapist* and the *trainer* ensure that the players are fit. They attend to injuries during matches.

**Liverpool's team back-up watch a match from the dug-out.**

# BALL CONTROL

Learning to control the ball with your feet is the starting point of soccer. Good ball control allows you to get your head up so that you can see where and when to pass the ball. Too much enthusiasm and not enough control, and the ball is easily lost to the other team.

The picture below shows the parts of the foot that can be used for kicking.

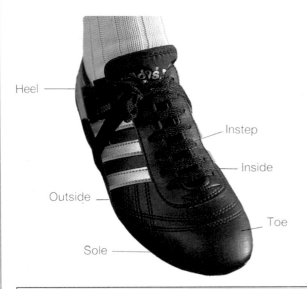

Heel

Instep

Inside

Outside

Toe

Sole

**Remember:**
Most people find it easier to kick with one foot than the other. However, you should practise using your weak foot as well as your strong one, because the ball might come to either foot during a game.

## Ball touch

Try these exercises, called ball touch, to help you get the feel of the ball.

1 Stand with one foot resting lightly on the ball. Jump so that your feet swap positions. See if you can do this exercise ten times in a row without stopping.

2 Roll the ball backwards, forwards and sideways under one foot. Practise until you can do it ten times with each foot without losing control.

3 Stand on your toes with your feet about 30cm apart and the ball between them. Jump lightly from one foot to the other, swinging your legs from side to side to tap the middle of the ball. Build up to 20 taps.

## First passes

The passes that you will find most useful at the start are with the inside of your foot for short distances, and the instep for more power. You can also use the outside of your foot for short, quick passes.

As most passes are made when the ball is moving, practise with a friend or against a wall.

### Instep pass

With your supporting foot alongside the ball, swing your kicking foot towards the ball with your toes pointing down.

Hit the ball with the top of your foot where your laces are.

Keep your knee over the ball as you kick and follow through towards the target.

### Inside foot pass

1 Place the supporting foot alongside the ball so that it points the way you want the ball to go.

2 Turn your kicking foot outwards and hit the middle of the ball with the broadest part of the inside of your foot.

3 Follow through with your kicking foot in the direction of the pass, so the ball moves smoothly and rolls forward.

## Practising passing

1 Practise passing to a friend, standing about 5m away. Start by using the inside of your foot, and then the outside.

When the ball comes to you, stop it with the sole of your foot (see "Wedge trap" on page 16). Then pass the ball back.

2 Start moving around, keeping about the same distance apart and continuing to pass the ball using one touch to control it first.

Now pass into the space to the side of your partner rather than straight to him. To help each other, hold out your arm to show which direction you are moving in and want the ball passed to, as shown above.

3 Either you or your friend can carry on having one touch to control the ball and one to pass it, while the other tries to return the ball with no controlling touch. This is called a first-time pass. Change over after a few minutes.

## Passing in a team

With a group of friends, try playing a sort of pig-in-the-middle game. Take it in turns to play in the middle as a defender, with the others spread out around the area of play. It is more difficult to pass with a defender nearby. You must act quickly, and look around to see who to pass to.

## Wall practice

Find a wall where you can practise, well away from any windows. Chalk a line on it, about 50cm above the ground. Stand 4m away and kick the ball below the line using inside foot passes and instep passes.

# RECEIVING AND CONTROLLING

In a soccer game the ball will not usually come conveniently to your feet at the right speed for you to run with it or pass it straight away. You will normally have to get it under control first. To start with, learn how to get the ball under control on the ground. This is done by either trapping or cushioning the ball.

## The wedge trap

This is useful when you are learning to receive passes and control the ball. It is an easy way to control a ball rolling along the ground. As the ball approaches, get yourself in line behind it and lift up the sole of your foot to stop it. See right.

The first passing exercise on page 15 shows how to practise this skill. Otherwise, you could kick the ball against a wall and trap it as it returns.

## Cushioning the ball

Cushioning the ball is a more advanced way to control an approaching pass than a wedge trap. It leaves the ball in front of you, ready to be kicked. Cushioning can be used for balls in the air as well as on the ground.

The secret of cushioning is to react as the ball hits you by relaxing and pulling back the part of your body which it strikes. This takes the speed off the ball so that it stops quickly or drops softly down in front of you.

**For the wedge trap hold your arms out for balance as your foot reaches out towards the ball.**

16

## Practising cushioning

1 With a friend, use the inside of your foot to pass to each other. Control the ball by cushioning it with the inside of your foot before passing back. Move on to controlling with one foot and passing with the other.

2 Drop the ball onto the top of your foot so that it is cushioned slightly and bounces about 30cm off your foot into the air. Catch it again before it hits the ground.

3 Get a friend to throw the ball to you so you can practise cushioning the ball in the air. Try it with your feet, thighs and chest.

Use the inside of your foot if the ball is on the ground or bouncing low.

The top of your foot is used for controlling balls that are dropping down. Bend your knee to bring your receiving foot up under the ball.

To cushion a dropping ball with your thigh lift your leg up with the knee bent. As the ball hits your thigh let your leg relax and drop slightly.

To control balls in the air with your chest, bend your knees with your legs apart and arch your back. Withdraw and relax your chest as the ball strikes.

# DRIBBLING

Dribbling is running with the ball under close control to get past a defender. You need to be able to change speed and direction very quickly. Dribblers use tricks to confuse and unbalance defenders and disguise the direction in which they intend to move.

Although you may find it difficult to start with, it is worth practising hard at this most exciting part of the game as it will give you as much satisfaction as scoring.

**England's Peter Beardsley moves past Denmark's Ivan Nielsen, keeping the ball under close control, Copenhagen 1989.**

**Dribbling tips:**
• Never let the ball get too far away or you may lose it, but do not keep it right under your feet either, or you will not be able to get your head up.

• Always look up to see where you are going and where the other players are. You should only glance down from time to time to check where the ball is.

## How to start dribbling

The best way to learn how to dribble is by moving around with the ball using lots of touches. Use the inside of your foot, by the big toe, then the outside, by the little toe, to produce a zig-zag movement of the ball.

1 Dribble in a straight line between two markers placed about 10m apart. Use the outside and inside or sole of your foot.

## Beating a defender

The pictures to the right show you how to approach and get past a defender. Make sure that you approach at a steady, controlled pace. This will allow you to choose which side to pass on, and the defender will have to guess which side you will go.

As you reach the defender you can make a feint or disguised move, called a dummy, to make your opponent go the wrong way.

2 Set up a line of six to eight markers, each about 2m apart. Dribble down the line, weaving in and out of them. Time yourself to see how much you can speed up, or set up two courses and race against friends.

3 With three or four friends, dribble balls in an area about 10 × 10m, marked out with objects at the corners. Control your own ball but try to knock others out of the area. See who is left in last.

◀ 1 The attacker approaches the defender and he makes it look as if he will pass on the left.

2 As the defender moves in to intercept the ball, the attacker quickly pushes the ball to the right with the outside of his foot. Before the defender recovers his balance, the attacker accelerates past.     ▶

# HEADING

Learning how to head the ball is very useful for scoring goals. You also use heading as a way to clear the ball from close to your own goal when you are defending and as a means of passing. It is not as dangerous or difficult as it looks if you do it the right way, and use a light ball or balloon to begin with.

1 Lean back from the waist as you prepare to head. Your neck should be firm to give you as much power as possible when you hit the ball.

2 As the ball approaches, drive forward and hit it with your forehead. Keep your eyes open as long as possible and watch the ball closely.

## How to start heading

This exercise will help you to get used to using your forehead.

1 Kneel down, drop the ball onto your forehead and try to head it up so that you can catch it. See if you can do it five times before you lose control.

2 With a friend, stand about two strides apart and take turns to head the ball to each other. One of you throws the ball; the other heads it back.

## Heading into goal

If you do not have a goal you can use, mark a chalk goal on a wall or mark goalposts on the ground. Take it in turns with a partner to be goalkeeper and attacker. The goalkeeper throws the ball to the attacker, who dives forward to head the ball into the goal.

## Heading when jumping

It is much more difficult to head the ball when you are jumping up to reach it but it is very useful in a full-size game. By jumping you will be more sure of getting to the ball before an opponent. If you are heading for a goal it is important to jump early in order to get above the ball to head it downwards. Practise heading while jumping once you are more confident of heading from a standing position.

## Head tennis

**Wimbledon's John Fashanu beats Luton Town's Steve Foster during their F.A. Cup semi-final match 1988.**

Head tennis is used by professional footballers as a fun way of practising heading. The ball must not bounce more than once before being headed back over the net.

# GOAL SCORING

Scoring is the aim of soccer. Every player can score but the main goal scorers are called strikers. Strikers need to be able to shoot accurately and act quickly and they should take every possible opportunity to shoot, even though they are unlikely to score every time.

## How to shoot

Striking the ball accurately is much more important than just kicking it hard. You will not often have the whole width of the goal to aim at with no goalkeeper in the way, so you are often shooting at a very small target.

Low shots are better than high shots because it is harder for a goalkeeper to bend or dive for a low ball than to jump to reach a high one. Also, low shots may deflect off another player or hit small bumps on the ground and so not go quite where the goalkeeper expects them to.

### Shooting tips:
• Use both feet when you practise kicking at goal. When you are shooting in a game you will not always have time to choose your best foot so you must be used to using both.

• Don't forget to follow your shot in, in case you could score from a rebound.

Use the same action for a low shot as for an instep pass (see page 14). Place your standing foot close to the ball and, keeping your eyes on the ball, get a good swing at it and follow through with your kicking leg.

## Shooting practice against a wall

For these exercises, you need to chalk a goal about your own height on a wall.

1 With the ball stationary, shoot at the goal and see if you can get five goals in a row. Move to the left and try scoring from an angle; then move to the right. Use a variety of angles and both feet.

2 Kick a ball at the goal and as it rebounds aim to score first time without a controlling touch. Practise this with a friend, playing alternate shots. See how many you can score.

3 With a friend, take turns to be goalkeeper and shooter. The goalkeeper feeds the ball to the shooter, who is allowed one touch to control the ball and one kick to shoot at goal.

## Shooting at a goal

These practice moves are for three or more players. You will need to mark out two goal posts before you start.

One player is the goalkeeper and another, (player A) stands about 15m in front of the goal. The others line up a little further back from goal. Take it in turns to be the goalkeeper and player A.

1 Each player in turn rolls the ball to A, who returns it with an inside foot pass.

2 When the player receives the ball back, he runs on to the ball and shoots at goal.

# DEFENDING

Defenders aim to win the ball back from the opposing team or at least clear it away from near their own goal so that opponents do not score.

If you have tried out the practices earlier on in this book, you will have already begun to learn how to intercept passes or tackle the player with the ball. To defend, you need to use these skills, along with another, called jockeying. Jockeying means putting pressure on your opponent so he makes a mistake and loses control of the ball, giving you the chance to win it.

When you challenge a player, you may jockey him, jockey and then tackle him, or tackle him straight away. Only tackle when you are sure you can win the ball. Knowing when to tackle is something that comes with experience.

## Jockeying

The idea of jockeying is to close in on your opponent, slowing him down and forcing him away from the route to goal. It should also make it difficult for him to pass or dribble.

While you do this, team-mates have time to position themselves around you to help defend. If you fail, they are then well-placed to make further challenges for the ball.

**England's John Barnes moves past Albania's Lekbello, during a World Cup qualifier, 1989.**

When jockeying an opponent, stand about a metre in front, sideways on and slightly to one side of him. This way he has no room to move and cannot pass the ball or run with it.

## Positioning for defence

Defenders need to be fast and be able to sense where the ball is likely to go next. They must also work well with their team-mates, so they can each judge where best to position themselves to hold off an attack.

## Practising defence

In addition to the exercises on page 15 and page 18, you could try the following. For these, you will need to mark out a small pitch about 20 × 10m with a small goal at each end, using clothing or other objects to mark the corners and goal posts:

1 Play a game with one friend so that you are both shooting and defending. See who can be first to get five goals. The one who scores most is also likely to be the best at defending!

2 Play number 1, but ask another friend to join in, so that it is two against one defender. The defender can now practise intercepting as well as jockeying to win the ball.

## Clearing the ball

In a crowded goal area defenders often need to clear the ball quickly. Try to volley the ball high and wide out towards the touchline and away from the danger area. Avoid passes that go across the penalty area.

**Italy's Gianluigi Galbagini clears the ball under pressure from England's Paul Rideout.**

# GOALKEEPING

The goalkeeper's task is to keep the ball out of the goal. He is the only player allowed to use his hands (apart from players making a throw-in – see page 30). One mistake by the goalkeeper can cost his team the match, so he has a lot of responsibility.

As well as being the last line of defence between the opposing team and the goal, the goalkeeper is also the first line of attack – throwing, kicking or rolling the ball to his team-mates to clear it away from goal. Experienced goalkeepers also organize their team's defence, calling instructions to team-mates about where to position themselves or which opponent to mark.

The most important requirement for a goalkeeper is to be able to catch the ball firmly with both hands. This is often known as having "safe hands".

## Saving Goals

Make sure your body is behind the ball, not just your hands. Your feet should be about shoulder-width apart to give you good balance.

To catch a low ball, get your hands round it with your fingers spread out so that your little fingers nearly touch. Pull it into your chest or stomach to hold it firmly.

To catch a high ball get your hands behind it with your fingers spread out but this time your thumbs should be nearly touching.

## Practising making saves

The first skill to practise is catching, but it is a good idea to learn how to punch the ball away when a catch is impossible as shown by England goalkeeper Peter Shilton below.

1 Practise kicking a ball against a wall so that it bounces back high or ask a friend to throw the ball to you at various heights. Use both hands to catch it.

2 Ask a friend to roll the ball about 2m to the side of you. Practise dropping down to save it. Keep your face and chest turned forwards, not downwards, as you dive sideways.

## Clearing the ball

A goalkeeper can clear the ball away from goal by throwing, kicking or rolling it. A short throw at shoulder height is good for clearing the ball quickly, before the opposing forwards have had time to retreat.

To clear the ball over the heads of opponents, you can kick the ball from your hands, as shown.

Throw the ball a little way up in front of you and kick it with your instep as it drops down.

Make sure you follow through with your kicking leg.

# THE LADDER TO THE TOP

Many people who start playing soccer dream of one day playing for a big club.

Remember that the harder you work at training and fitness, the better your chances are of becoming a professional.

From the age of seven or eight there should be lots of opportunities to play football at school, cubs or your local sports centre, which may run coaching sessions.

Soccer clubs employ scouts to talent-spot boys from the age of eleven. If you are spotted you may be asked to attend a Centre of Excellence and become a club associate schoolboy.

After his school career, an associate schoolboy may become a trainee professional, playing for his club's youth team and doing jobs such as boot-cleaning.

At the age of eighteen, a club may sign up a trainee as a full professional. At first, the new player will probably play in the reserve team until he is chosen for the first team.

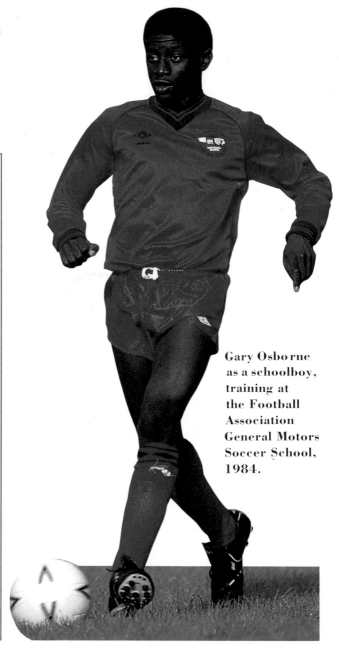

Gary Osborne as a schoolboy, training at the Football Association General Motors Soccer School, 1984.

## Life as a professional

A professional player has a very busy week. The first team plays one or two matches every week during the soccer season from September to May. They usually have two days off a week, and have a strict timetable of training on other days. Every player must keep fit and continue to practise his soccer skills.

The playing life of a professional is fairly short. Most retire at the age of 30 to 34, but goalkeepers often stay until they are 40.

Quite a few players go into soccer management after retirement. In a few cases, experienced professionals become player-managers towards the end of their playing careers.

**England goalkeepers, Chris Woods and Peter Shilton, go through a training routine during a pre-world-cup training session, 1986.**

# LAWS OF THE GAME

A soccer match is controlled by a referee, who makes sure that the players stick to the 17 laws of the game. The referee is assisted by two linesmen, who stand on opposite touchlines. Each linesman has a flag which he uses to signal to the referee, for example, when the ball goes over the touchline.

Whenever a player commits a foul (unfair play), the referee stops the game and gives possession of the ball to the other team.

## Free kicks

A free kick is taken at the spot where a foul took place. There are nine fouls, such as handling the ball and pushing, kicking or tripping an opponent, for which a direct free kick is awarded (you can score from this). For less serious offences, such as being off-side, an indirect free kick is given (you cannot score directly from this).

## Penalty kicks

If a foul takes place inside the penalty area, for which the referee would give a direct free kick, a penalty is awarded. Only the goalkeeper and the player taking the penalty are involved. The player shoots from the penalty spot and the goalkeeper tries to make a save.

## Throw-ins

A throw-in is used to get the ball back in play after it has crossed the touchline. It is a two-handed throw over the head, with both feet on or behind the touch-line.

**A referee can book or send a player off for a serious offence.**

**Neil McDonald of Everton takes a throw-in.**

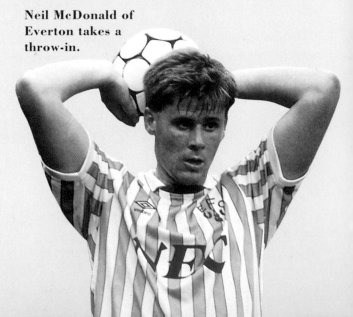

## Corner kicks

A corner kick is given when the ball has crossed the goal-line and was last touched by a defending player. The player taking the corner can score directly from his kick. The defenders must stand at least 9.15m away from the ball until it has been kicked.

## Goal kicks

These are given when the attacking players have sent the ball over the goal-line outside the goal posts. The ball is placed inside the goal area, and the kick is usually taken by the goalkeeper. The ball must be kicked outside the penalty area.

## The off-side rule

A player is in an off-side position if he is in the opponents' half of the pitch and there are less than two opponents between him and the goal-line.

The referee will decide if a player is off-side when the ball is played forward by one of his team. If the off-side player is not interfering with play the referee may let the game go on.

**A player who is not off-side as he has two opponents between himself and the goal.**

**A player off-side. The referee would stop the game and award an indirect free kick.**

# INDEX

William Collins Sons & Co. Ltd.
London · Glasgow · Sydney · Auckland
Toronto · Johannesburg

First published in Great Britain 1990

© William Collins Sons & Co Ltd 1990

A CIP catalogue record for this book is available from the British Library

ISBN 0 00 190014-5 HB
      0 00 191215-1 PB

PHOTO ACKNOWLEDGEMENTS

The publishers thank Bob Thomas Sports Photography for permission to reproduce the photographs on the following pages:
2, 3, 5, 9, 18 left, 21 bottom left, 24 bottom right, 25 bottom right, 27 left, 28, 29, 30.